THE STORY OF CHOCOLATE

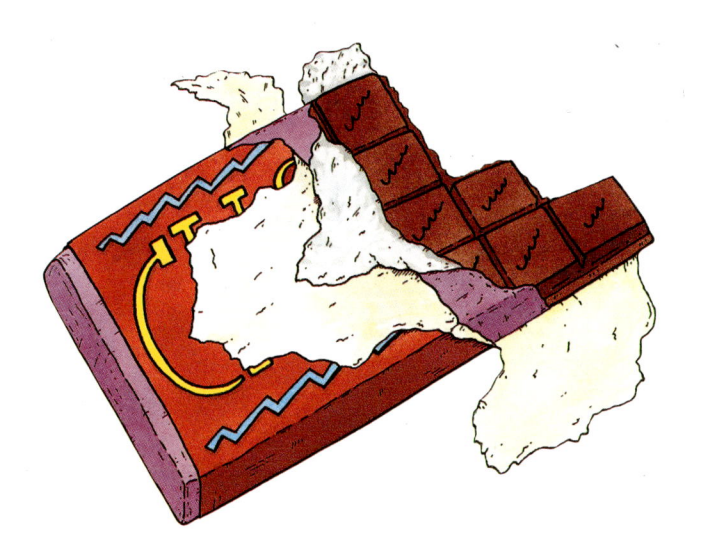

Written by John Eden
Illustrated by Nick Duffy

CollinsEducational
An Imprint of HarperCollins*Publishers*

Contents

Introduction	3
Voyages of Discovery	4
Cortes and the Aztecs	6
Chocolate in Europe	10
Chocolate comes to England	12
A Chocolate Giant	16
From Pod to Product	22
A Chocolate Assortment	29
A Taste of Chocolate	30
Index	32

Introduction

This book is for anyone who enjoys chocolate. In the United Kingdom, that means most people – nineteen out of every twenty of us, according to surveys of eating habits. These reveal that, on average, each person in the UK eats about 250 grams of chocolate every week. That's roughly equal to four Mars Bars, or five large KitKats, or five small bars of Cadbury's Dairy Milk.

The Story of Chocolate is about the history and manufacture of this popular substance. The history starts with the Maya and Aztecs of Central America, who many centuries ago enjoyed a drink they called *xocolatl* and traded goods for cocoa beans. In the 16th century, Spanish explorers discovered the Aztec civilisation and took stolen Aztec gold back home with them to Spain. They also took cocoa beans and thereby introduced drinking chocolate to Europe.

Eventually, new processes were discovered that enabled cocoa beans to be turned into the range of products we know today. The book explains how chocolate is made and how the industry has grown from small beginnings into the huge international companies that produce one of our favourite tastes.

Voyages of Discovery

More than three-and-a-half thousand years ago, the Egyptians began investigating what lay southwards down the river Nile and northwards into Assyria. Their neighbours, the Phoenicians, were also great travellers, sailing around the Mediterranean to Greece, Italy and Spain, and even as far as Cornwall and the Isles of Scilly in search of the precious commodity, tin. This was vital for making alloys which would be used for creating tools, weapons and everyday items.

The Phoenicians were only one of many trading nations, and at this time a great number of sea and land routes were opening up across the world. One of the most famous of these led to chocolate being brought to Europe. This was the Silk Road, an overland route that had been used since the 2nd century AD, when the Roman Empire traded with

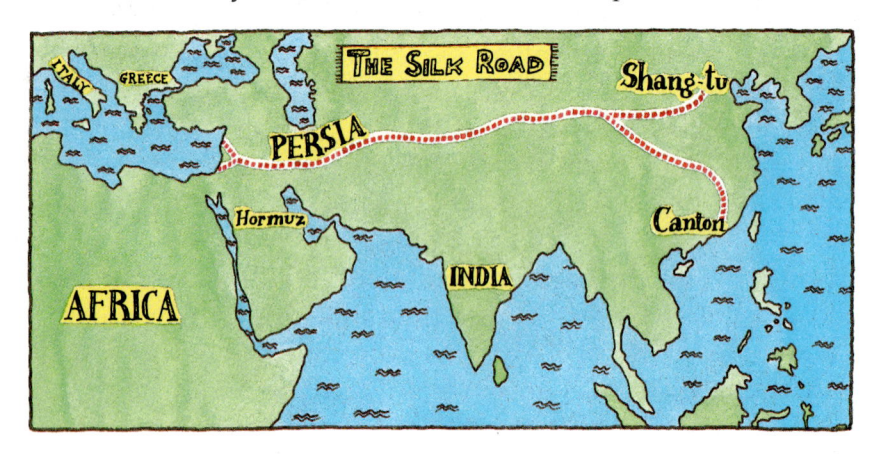

The Silk Road was a famous overland trade route

the Chinese. Apart from silk, many other prized goods were brought back to Europe along the Silk Road – pepper, ginger, spices, dyes and cotton – and the trade went on for more than a thousand years. However, by the 14th century, things had changed. The Mongols, who had conquered Northern China and had been happy to let Western merchants through, were themselves driven out by the Chinese, and the old trade routes became dangerous.

Once the land routes were declared unsafe, sailors began searching for a sea route to China. They sailed east, in the same direction as the Silk Road, but were unable to find a route. Then an Italian sailor called Christopher Columbus decided to try sailing west, because as the world is round, he had worked out he could keep going until he came to China. Queen Isabella of Castile gave Columbus money to buy ships and supplies for the voyage and in 1492 he crossed the Atlantic Ocean, landing not in India as he thought, but in what is now called the West Indies.

After this first voyage, Columbus crossed the Atlantic three more times, and the way to the East seemed clear. Spanish ships began to cross the ocean in search of trade and the gold and silver rumoured to be there for the taking. Although the Spaniards searched all over this new territory and explored around 11 000kms of coastline, it was 20 years before they saw any results. Then, at last, a man called Hernan Cortes succeeded in bringing home to Spain treasures such as gold and silver, and eventually, cocoa beans. He later became known as the man who introduced the beans to Europe, although Christopher Columbus had previously brought them to the court of King Ferdinand. At the time, however, they were thought to be useless.

Cortes and the Aztecs

Long before Cortes began his journeys, an ancient race of people called the Maya were living in Central America. Their civilisation and knowledge were highly developed. They had a system of writing which they used to set down their ideas about astronomy, history and religion. They were good mathematicians, too, with ideas that were, for many centuries, well ahead of those in Europe. The Maya were also farmers, and one of their crops was the *cacao* tree. The name comes from two Mayan words meaning 'bitter juice', because of the taste of the drink made from the beans. It is thought that English importers mixed up the spelling years ago, and *cacao* eventually became *cocoa*.

Map of Central America

Cocoa beans were used as symbols for numbers by the Mayans

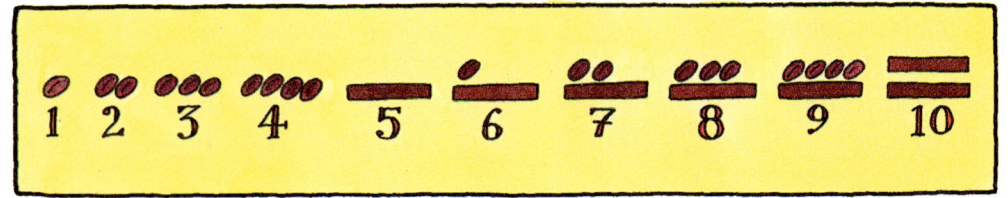

To the west of the Yucatan Peninsula, which was the land of the Maya, lived a people called the Aztecs. They, too, had a well-developed civilisation which was centred on their capital city of Tenochtitlan. The Aztecs had strong armies, and they had defeated many of their neighbouring tribes. These defeated people had to pay a kind of tax to the Aztecs, known as *tribute*. This tribute included clothing, jewellery, animal skins – and cocoa beans. The climate in Aztec lands was too dry for cocoa trees to grow, so as well as demanding them in tribute,

The Aztec cocoa bean exchange rate

they traded their own goods in exchange for cocoa beans. The beans were so highly prized that in Central America they came to be used as money.

There were many rumours that Montezuma, the Aztec emperor, lived in a castle made of solid gold, slept in a gold bed and ate from gold plates. So, in 1517, Cortes set sail from Cuba with 600 men to find this fabulous treasure. On the coast of the Gulf of Mexico he founded the city of Vera Cruz. He then ordered his ships to be burned, to show his men that there would be no going back until they had completed their mission.

Cortes expected to have to fight his way to Montezuma, but, by a strange chance, he was invited to meet the emperor. This was due to an ancient Aztec legend about the god Quetzalcoatl. It was said that he had given away to human beings some of the secrets of the gods – for example, how to read the stars and how to use a calendar – and had also given them the seeds of the cocoa tree, from the Garden of Life.

Quetzalcoatl was punished by another god for his generosity. His powers were taken from him, and he was banished. Before leaving, he vowed that one day he would return from the East after journeying overseas. Montezuma's messengers reported that the Spaniards had come over the sea from the East, and so the emperor thought that Cortes and his men might have been sent by Quetzalcoatl, and received them at his royal palace. Here, Cortes first tasted the highly prized drink made from cocoa beans known to the Aztecs as *xocolatl* (pronounced 'zoh-kol-atal'). One of Cortes' soldiers, a young man called Bernal Diaz de Castilo, kept a diary of his adventures and described the drinking of xocolatl like this:

Montezuma's food was served on red and black plates. While he was eating, the guards in the nearby rooms did not dare to make a noise or speak above a whisper. Sometimes they brought him, in cups of solid gold, a drink made from the cocoa plant. I saw them bring in fifty large jugs of this chocolate, all frothed up, of which he would drink a little. They always served it with great reverence...
There were Indians who told him jokes, and others who sang and danced, for Montezuma was very fond of music and entertainment and rewarded his entertainers with the remains of the food and chocolate.

Cortes himself wrote about xocolatl and its wonderful properties:

One cup of this precious drink allows a man to go a whole day without taking nourishment.

Hernan Cortes

The initial meetings between Cortes and Montezuma were polite – but the peace didn't last. The Spaniards took Montezuma hostage and forced him to make the Aztecs obey Spanish rule. Not surprisingly, the Aztecs rebelled, and in 1520 drove Cortes and his men out of Tenochtitlan – but not before the Spanish had put Montezuma to death. In 1521, Cortes returned and destroyed Tenochtitlan, and with it the Aztec empire. The Spaniards completely rebuilt the ruined capital and renamed it Mexico City. The treasures of the Aztecs were now there for the taking and, in due course, Cortes set sail for Spain in ships loaded with gold, silver, precious jewels and cocoa beans. His ships sailed back via Africa, where he stopped to plant young cocoa trees. Cortes knew that the parts of the coast between what is now called the Ivory Coast and Nigeria had the hot, wet conditions that cocoa trees need, because Spanish and Portuguese sailors had already explored the area.

In Spain, the chocolate drink was introduced to the royal court. It was flavoured with sugar and vanilla, or other spices, and became as popular with Spanish nobility as it had been with the Maya and the Aztecs. So popular, that the Spanish were determined to keep the knowledge of chocolate drinking to themselves. They managed to keep the secret for almost a hundred years.

Chocolate in Europe

European travellers to the New World of Central America discovered chocolate drinking in the same way that Columbus and Cortes had. An Italian, Giralamo Benzoni, first tried the drink there in 1542. He didn't think much of it at first: in fact, he said it was *'more suitable for pigs than men.'* He seems to have had second thoughts, though, because he wrote later:

Chocolate drinking became very popular

When I passed through a village, if an Indian wished to give me some chocolate, he was very surprised to see me refuse it, and went away laughing. But eventually... I did as others did. The flavour is rather bitter, but it satisfies and refreshes the body.

Travellers like Giralamo took the news of chocolate back to their own countries, but the secret was already leaking out of Spain. In 1606 another Italian, Antonio Carletti, visited Spain and when he returned to Italy took with him a recipe for the drink. Even so, it took time for the taste to catch on, and it was another hundred years before the coffee houses of Venice and Florence became famous across Europe for the chocolate that the rich – especially fashionable ladies – were flocking to drink.

In France, Anne of Austria, the daughter of the King of Spain, married King Louis XIII in 1615. She brought with her to the royal court her own supply of chocolate and a maid to mix it for her. In 1659 King Louis XIV gave royal permission to David Chalion of Paris *'to sell and deliver in all towns and other places of the kingdom a certain composition called chocolat'*. When the same King became engaged to his future wife Maria Theresa, her engagement present to him was a fine jewellery box filled with chocolate.

King Louis XIV of France

Chocolate drinking came to Switzerland in 1697, when Heinrich Escher, the mayor of Zurich, returned from a trip to Belgium bringing word of the new taste he had discovered there. Chocolate appeared in Germany at about the same time, and by 1714 Frederick I of Prussia had even put a tax on the drink. His son, King Frederick the Great, was a famous general who also wrote music and poetry. He enjoyed chocolate too, but it seems that he wasn't happy about the cost of cocoa beans. In 1747 he paid a chemist to experiment with lime tree leaves in an attempt to make a cheap drink that would taste like chocolate. The result tasted dreadful, and was never heard of again.

Chocolate comes to England

Spanish galleons sailing home across the Atlantic carrying treasures from the New World were often attacked by English ships, out to steal their cargoes. Sir Francis Drake was so successful in taking Spanish gold that his ship – *The Pelican* – was renamed *Golden Hind*. But although the English sailors were delighted to steal gold from the Spaniards they had a low opinion of cocoa beans. An English monk, Thomas Gage, wrote in 1548: *'When we have taken a good prize, a ship laden with cocoa, in anger and wrath we have hurled overboard this good commodity not regarding the worth and goodness of it, but calling it in bad Spanish cagarutta de carnero, or sheep dung in good English.'*

The Golden Hind

The English didn't go on thinking of cocoa beans as sheep dung, though. Just over a hundred years after Thomas Gage wrote the passage above, there appeared what is believed to be the first printed advertisement for chocolate in England. It was in a 1657 edition of a paper called the *Public Advertiser* and it read: *'In Bishopsgate Street, in Queens Head Alley, at a Frenchman's house, is an excellent West India drink called Chocolate to be sold, where you may have it ready at any time, and also unmade at reasonable rates.'* The Frenchman's rates were probably only reasonable in

FASCINATING FACT

10 000 000 000 Smarties (that's ten billion) are eaten every year in the United Kingdom.

comparison with other chocolate prices, because although the drink was becoming as popular in England as it was in other countries in Europe, it was still a taste that only the rich could afford. The court of King Charles II enjoyed chocolate, and Samuel Pepys, an admiralty official and member of parliament, wrote about chocolate in his famous diary. He describes several visits to coffee houses (where chocolate was served), and even suggests that chocolate might be good for a hangover. On the coronation day of King Charles, 23 April 1661, Pepys celebrated by having far too much to drink, but describes how the next morning he went to a coffee house where he had… *'chocolate to settle my stomach.'*

It was not long before special chocolate houses opened, and became very popular. The best known London houses were The Chocolate Tree and White's. White's opened in 1693, and is a famous club to this day. Both of these houses were

White's Chocolate House, London

meeting places for distinguished writers, lawyers and politicians. In 1709, Sir Richard Steele wrote in the first edition of his magazine *The Tatler* that *'All accounts of gallantry, pleasure and entertainment shall be under the article of White's Chocolate House.'*

An old-fashioned grocer's store

The drink that was served in these houses was made from solid blocks of chocolate imported from France and Spain, as until 1728 there was no cocoa bean processing plant in England. But as more and more chocolate was consumed throughout Europe, more cocoa trees were planted in the tropics to keep up with the demand.

More trees meant more cocoa beans coming on to the market, resulting in falling prices. Chocolate became cheaper, and more people could afford to buy it. This growth of sales encouraged business people to look into the possibilities of dealing in chocolate, and in England chemists and grocers were amongst those who tried their hand at the new skills. Chemists were interested because chocolate was thought to be health-giving, and chocolate-coated pills and chocolate lozenges became good sellers.

The milk used in making Dairy Milk chocolate in one year would fill nearly 14.5 Olympic-size swimming pools.

Joseph Fry, who opened the first English cocoa bean processing factory in Bristol in 1728, was a chemist, as was Joseph Terry, the founder of the York-based chocolate company. Grocers were accustomed to buying foods and other goods from abroad, and so found it easy enough to add cocoa to their imports. In York, grocer Isaac Rowntree became a chocolate manufacturer, and in 1824, a shop opened at 93 Bull Street, in Birmingham centre. At first, the owner dealt in tea and coffee, but after several years he began buying and experimenting with cocoa beans.

The owner's name was John Cadbury.

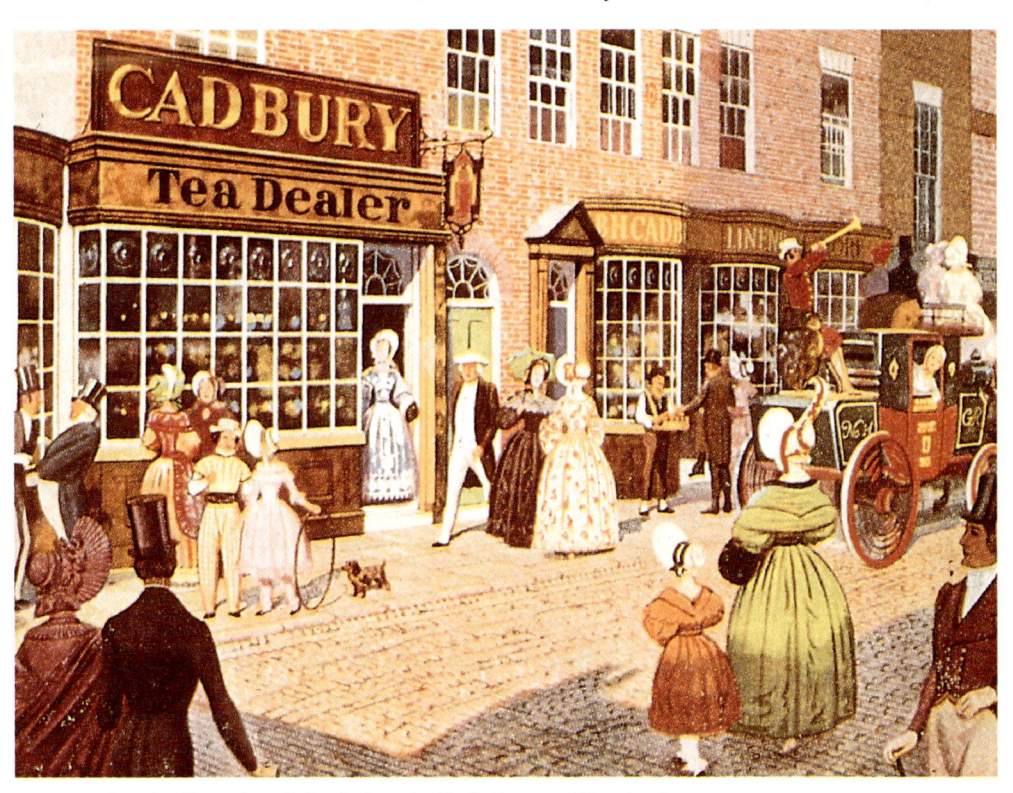

John Cadbury's original shop in Bull Street, Birmingham

A Chocolate Giant

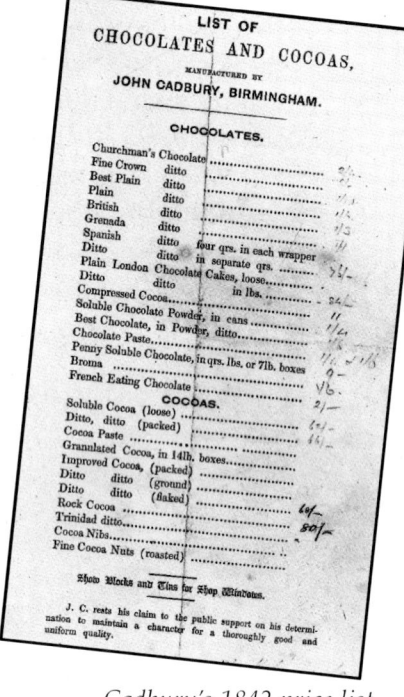

John Cadbury was the founder of what was to become the United Kingdom's biggest and most famous chocolate company. By 1831 he had rented a warehouse near the Bull Street shop, where he began grinding cocoa beans and concocting his own recipes for drinking chocolate which he sold in the shop. Sales of chocolate were low, and although his 1842 price list shows a wide range of chocolate products, tea and coffee were still his best-selling lines.

In 1855, John's wife Candia died, and he never seemed to get over the shock. His brother Benjamin had joined him in 1847 to help develop the business, and the Cadbury brothers became famous as Queen Victoria's chocolate suppliers. But despite this, John's heart was no longer in the work, and profits began to fall.

Cadbury's 1842 price list

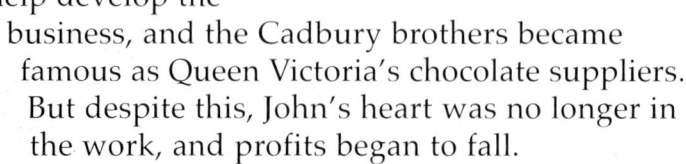

John Cadbury retired in 1861 and the business was taken over by his sons, George and Richard. In 1866 they made a discovery that was to set them on the road to success. George went to visit the Van Houten

George Cadbury

chocolate factory in Holland, and came back with a new machine that would squeeze out all of the cocoa butter from cocoa beans. Cocoa butter is an oily substance found in the beans, and it had always been a problem for chocolate makers, as it made the drink rather heavy and greasy. To solve the problem, manufacturers added flour or potato starch to the cocoa powder. This would soak up the cocoa butter, but it didn't do much for the taste of the chocolate. The taste was even worse when some chocolate makers added brick dust or finely ground rust to their product. But the Cadbury brothers' new press produced a cocoa powder that was free of cocoa butter. They called it Cocoa Essence, and it was very much like the cocoa powder of today. George and Richard, excited by this breakthrough, advertised Cocoa Essence in newspapers and magazines. They sent samples to doctors and chemists, who reported that it was a pure and healthy food. All this publicity helped sales to grow, and Cocoa Essence became Cadbury's most important product.

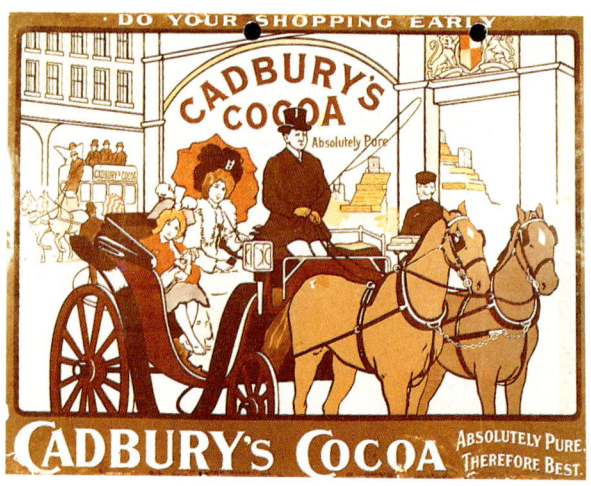

An early advertisement for Cadbury's cocoa

Finding an easy way to extract cocoa butter from the beans brought about another important development. Drinking chocolate was made by dissolving blocks of solid cocoa in water, and it is very likely that people nibbled at these blocks. The powdery, bitter taste would have been nothing like the chocolate of today, because an important part of eating chocolate production is the addition of extra cocoa butter to the solid cocoa. Once that discovery was made, the way was clear to producing chocolate in solid bars, and manufacturers began to make many different kinds. They soon began producing assorted cream chocolates in attractive boxes, too.

For many years the workers sat at large circular stones to cover and decorate chocolates

In 1875 the first milk chocolate was made. It was invented in Switzerland by Daniel Peter, who combined cocoa powder, sugar, cocoa butter and condensed milk – another Swiss product invented by Henri Nestlé. This milk chocolate was a great success in Britain, and the Cadbury brothers were determined to make their own version. In 1898 they launched a milk chocolate bar, but it didn't taste as good as the Swiss chocolate, and sales were poor. They tried different ways of blending the ingredients and different production methods, and George's son (also called George) was sent to Switzerland to look at their factories. At last, after much research, the Cadbury brothers were ready to sell their new milk chocolate.

The card box department at Cadbury's in 1905

It was made with fresh milk, rather than the powdered milk that some manufacturers used, and they wanted to choose a name that would make people think about this milky content. They came up with three ideas: Highland Milk Chocolate, Jersey Chocolate and Dairymaid Chocolate. The last name was chosen, but changed slightly, and in 1905 Cadbury's Dairy Milk Chocolate was launched. It was a huge success, and has remained Britain's most popular chocolate ever since.

Throughout the 20th century, chocolate manufacturers saw great advances in technology, transport, advertising and product ranges. The one-man business that started in the little Bull Street shop grew into a company with 128 individual production plants and 52 major plants, working 24 hours a day. The Cadbury family were Quakers, with strong religious beliefs, and they put their beliefs into practice from their earliest days in business. John Cadbury, the founder, worked hard to help to stop the Victorian custom of sending children up chimneys to clean them. His sons, George and Richard, helped adults from the Birmingham slums to learn to read, and they also gave a great deal of money to charity. But it is for the way they treated their workers that the Cadburys are best remembered.

In 1870, the Cadbury factory in the centre of Birmingham was no longer big enough to cope with growing trade. So the brothers found a new site, four miles south in open fields near a stream called Bourn Brook. They named the site Bournville, combining Bourn with 'ville', the French word for town. They did this because French chocolate was very popular, and they wanted their factory to sound French. The new factory in Bournville opened in 1879 and at the same time 16 houses were built for Cadbury's most senior workers. This was the start of Bournville village, which became famous as an example of good quality housing built

Workers' houses at Bournville village

20

for working people, and is still thriving today. At the same time, the Cadburys started a whole range of benefits for their workers that were far ahead of what any other employers - or the state - provided. There were pension schemes, medical help, cheap meals in the factory canteen, rewards for good time-keeping, a 5.5 -day week when workers elsewhere worked 6 days a week, and Bank Holiday closing. Cadbury had its own 'Day Continuation School', where workers who had left school at 14 – and most of them did that – could carry on with their studies. In return for all these benefits, workers were expected to reciprocate with loyalty and good conduct. Hence the factory girls became known locally as Cadbury Angels.

Above: Day Continuation class, 1915. Top: class with author's mother

From Pod to Product

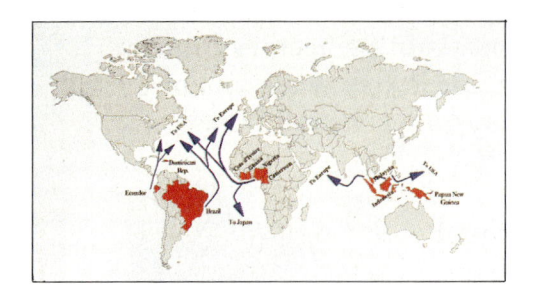

Map of cocoa-growing areas

Cocoa trees grow in tropical climates with steamy, humid conditions and periods of heavy rain. The world's main bean-producing areas are all in the tropics. The trees are bushy in shape and grow to a height of about 5m, although the very tallest can reach a height of just over 7m. The cocoa tree has pink blossoms which grow out of the trunk and lower branches. Eventually some of the blossoms turn into pods.

The pods are shaped like small, thin rugby balls. When they are ripe they are yellow and about 20cm long. Inside the pod are the cocoa beans, usually 30-40 in number and surrounded by a sweet white pulp. In West African countries, where the cocoa for UK chocolate comes from, each tree grows 20-30 pods in a year. There are two harvests, when the farmer visits his cocoa trees regularly to cut the ripe pods from the trees with machetes. Those that

Top: pods grow out of the trunk
Above: the split pod and beans

are very high in the trees are cut down with knives on long poles. The pods are then collected together and split open and the beans and pulp scooped out and heaped onto a layer of banana tree leaves. The heap of beans is then covered with more banana leaves, and the beans and pulp are left like this for about 6 days, to ferment. The heat of fermentation – about 50 degrees celsius – turns the beans brown, and the white pulp becomes a thin liquid that drains away.

The beans are then spread over wooden tables and left to dry thoroughly in the sun. The cocoa farmer rakes and turns the beans every so often and covers them up at night, or if rain seems likely. In countries where the weather is too wet to allow table drying, the beans are placed in metal dryers heated by oil-fired burners.

Beans drying on tables.

When the cocoa beans are dry, they are packed into sacks and taken to the buying station. At the station, a simple quality check is made on the beans. A sack is chosen at random, and 50 beans taken out and split to make 100 half-beans. The halves are then placed on a board divided into 100 squares, and inspected for quality.

The beans are transported by lorry to the ports

The bean sacks are then loaded into lorries and taken to the port to be shipped. When the beans arrive at the chocolate factories they are cleaned to remove dust, grit and stones, then roasted at 135 degrees celsius in large metal drums that look like giant tumble driers. This roasting develops the flavour of the beans, and also makes the shells more brittle so that after the beans have cooled they are more easily cracked open or 'kibbled'. The pieces of broken shell are 'winnowed', that is, blown away by jets of air, leaving the bean centres, called the 'nib'. The nib is passed through a series of grinding machines and ground until a liquid that looks like thick brown cream is produced. This liquid is cocoa liquor, and is the starting point for cocoa, dark chocolate and milk chocolate.

Cocoa

Cocoa liquor contains a fat called cocoa butter. It melts just below body temperature, which is why chocolate has such a pleasant creamy texture. Powerful presses are used to squeeze the butter out of the liquor, leaving a solid cake of cocoa powder. This is broken up, sieved, and weighed into tins as cocoa. Cocoa has rather a bitter taste, and sugar is usually added when it is made as a drink. Sometimes, finely ground sugar is added to the cocoa powder at the factory and the resulting product is sold as drinking chocolate.

The cocoa butter press

Cocoa powder cakes are ground to produce cocoa

Dark Chocolate

To make dark chocolate, cocoa liquor is mixed with sugar and extra cocoa butter and the resulting paste ground and well mixed for several hours, until the sugar crystals are reduced to the point where a very smooth liquid results. The proportions of sugar and cocoa butter added depend on whether the chocolate is to be moulded into bars or used to coat biscuits or chocolate assortment centres. After this first mixing, the liquid is stirred for many more hours in a large container called a 'conche'. The temperature in the conche, and the mixing time, are important in developing the final taste and texture of the chocolate.

Milk Chocolate

In the case of milk chocolate, the cocoa liquor is mixed with sugar and added to milk that has been evaporated – or sometimes milk powder – to make a rich, thick liquid. The resulting mixture is dried to make chocolate 'crumb', which is then ground into a fine powder. Extra cocoa butter (and sometimes extra cocoa liquor or sugar, depending on the taste required) is added to the powder to form a paste, which is then well mixed and processed in the same way as dark chocolate.

White Chocolate

White chocolate is made from cocoa butter, milk, sugar and vanilla. It is made in a similar way to milk chocolate, but the cocoa butter takes the place of cocoa liquor. White 'crumb' is produced in this process. The cocoa butter used in white chocolate has to have a mild flavour and so it is pressed from cocoa beans that have been very lightly roasted.

Tempering and Moulding

Before dark, milk or white chocolate can be made into bars or used as covering for centres, it must be 'tempered'. This process involves mixing and cooling under very careful conditions so that the final chocolate has certain properties. It should come out of the moulds easily, look shiny and attractive, snap sharply when it is broken, and keep well, without becoming dull or discoloured.

Tempering consists of heating the chocolate to 49-50 degrees celsius to make sure all the cocoa butter has melted, then stirring it carefully as it cools. Dark chocolate is cooled to 29 degrees, and milk and white chocolate to 28 degrees. If the chocolate is to have ingredients like fruit or nuts, they are warmed up to the same temperature as the chocolate, and added near the end of the tempering process.

The tempered chocolate is then used to coat centres, or is made into bars. The machines that make the bars may be as long as 30m and capable of handling several tonnes of chocolate every day. Conveyor belts on the machines hold brightly polished moulds which are filled from nozzles with the warm chocolate mixture. Because the mixture is not very runny, the moulds are shaken and vibrated so that the chocolate spreads and no air bubbles are trapped. The conveyor belt then takes the moulds further down the machine to be chilled, and the resulting solid chocolate bars are slipped from the moulds to be wrapped on high-speed automatic machines.

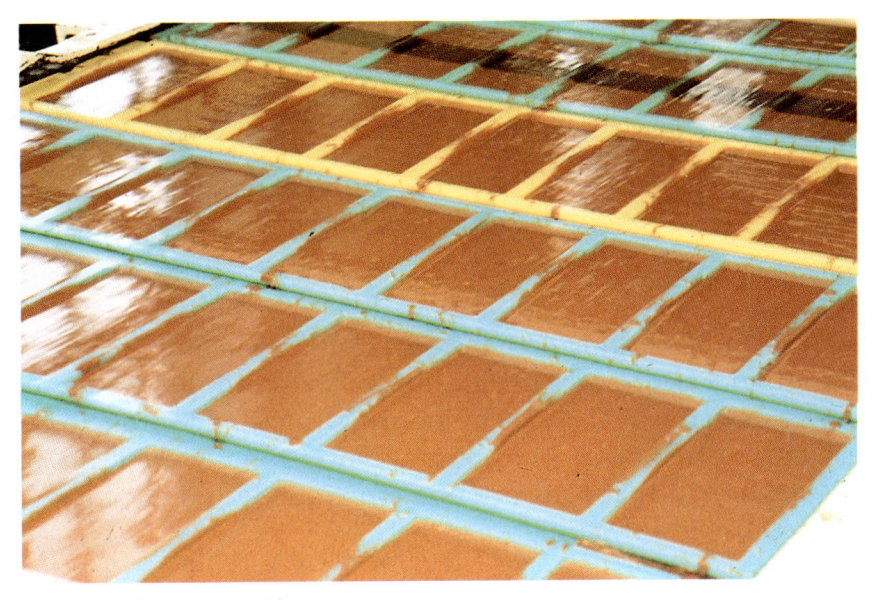

Chocolate bars in moulds

Chocolate Centres

The bars of chocolate described above are called 'moulded products'. The other important group of chocolate products consists of those where an outer chocolate layer

Confectionery centres about to go through the enrobing machine

covers a filling: chocolate biscuits, toffee bars and assortment chocolates, for example. These products are are made in two ways: either by pouring the filling into a chocolate shell or by sending the centres on a wire mesh conveyor belt that runs under a stream of liquid chocolate in an enrobing machine.

Finally, the chocolate products go out on sale to the public. It has been estimated that in the United Kingdom there are 250 000 places where chocolate can be bought, including 60 000 groceries and supermarkets, 40 000 sweetshops and newsagents, and thousands of corner shops, petrol stations, public houses, kiosks and vending machines.

A Chocolate Assortment
A chocolate calendar

The list below shows the years when some of Britain's most popular chocolate bars and assortments first appeared. Some products have been around for a surprisingly long time...

1866 Fry's Chocolate Cream
1905 Cadbury's Dairy Milk chocolate
1910 Cadbury's Bournville chocolate
1915 Cadbury's Milk Tray assortment
1920 Cadbury's Flake
1921 Cadbury's Fruit and Nut
1930 Cadbury's Whole Nut
   Fry's Crunchie
1932 Mars Bar
1933 Rowntree Black Magic assortment
1935 Mars Milky Way
   Rowntree Aero
   Rowntree Chocolate Crisp
   (now called KitKat)
1936 Mars Energy Balls
   (now called Maltesers)
   Mackintosh Quality Street assortment
   Rowntree Dairy Box assortment
1937 Rowntree Smarties
   Mackintosh Rolo
1938 Cadbury's Roses assortment
1951 Mars Bounty
1958 Mars Galaxy
1959 Mackintosh Caramac
1962 Mars Topic
   Rowntree After Eight mints
1967 Mars Marathon
   (now Snickers)
1968 Rowntree Matchmakers
1976 Rowntree Mackintosh Yorkie
1978 Cadbury's Double Decker
1980 Rowntree Mackintosh Drifter
1981 Cadbury's Wispa
1985 Mars M&Ms
1989 Nestlé Rowntree Secret

FASCINATING FACT

On average, 228 000 bars of Cadbury's chocolate are eaten every hour.

Note: In 1969, Rowntree and Mackintosh merged to become Rowntree Mackintosh Ltd., which became Rowntree plc in 1987. Soon after, in 1988, Nestlé SA bought Rowntree plc to form Nestlé Rowntree.

A Taste of Chocolate

Two easy recipes for you to try.

Chocolate Aztec

This is a recipe from Mexico, which gives some idea of how the Aztec and Mayan chocolate drinks tasted. Although this tastes far less bitter than the ancient drinks, sugar could still be added.

Ingredients:
100g plain dark chocolate
550ml skimmed milk
2–3 drops vanilla essence
a pinch of cinnamon
a pinch of ground cloves

Method:
Heat all the ingredients gently in a saucepan (but don't boil them) until the drink is hot and the chocolate has melted. Whisk up the liquid until there is a froth on the top and serve.

Crunchy Syrup Bars

Crunchy biscuits that don't need an oven.

Ingredients:
50g butter or margarine
200g plain dark chocolate
3 tablespoons golden syrup
220g wholemeal biscuits
icing sugar

Method:
Gently heat the butter, chocolate and syrup together in a small saucepan. Stir until everything has melted and mixed together. Crumble the wholemeal biscuits into small pieces and sprinkle them into the mixture, stirring well. Pour the mixture into a non-stick shallow tin about 20cm square and allow to cool. Refrigerate until set, which may take several hours. Remove the crunch layer from the tin and cut into fingers. Sprinkle each bar with a light coating of icing sugar.

Index

Africa	9	
Anne of Austria	11	
Aztecs	3, 6, 7, 8, 9, 30	

Benzoni, Giralomo 10
Bourn Brook 20
Bournville 20, 29

Cadbury, George
   16, 17, 19, 20
Cadbury, John 15, 16, 20
Cadbury, Richard
   16, 17, 19, 20
Cadbury factory 20, 21
Carletti, Antonio 10
Charles II 13
chocolate centres 27, 28
chocolate, dark
   24, 25, 26, 30, 31
chocolate, drinking
   3, 16, 18, 25
chocolate, milk
   14, 19, 24, 26, 29
Chocolate Tree, The 13
chocolate, white 26
Cocoa Essence 17
cocoa butter
   17, 18, 19, 25, 26
cocoa harvesting 22

Columbus, Christopher
   5, 10
Cortes, Hernan
   5, 6, 7, 8, 9, 10

Diaz, Bernal 8
Drake, Sir Francis 12

Egyptians 4
Escher, Heinrich 11

Frederick I 11
Frederick the Great 11
Fry, Joseph 15

Gage, Thomas 12
Golden Hind, The 12

Isabella, Queen 5
Ivory Coast 9

Louis XIII 11
Louis XIV 11

Maya 3, 6, 7, 9, 30
Mexico 7, 30
Mexico City 9
Mongols, The 5
Montezuma 7, 8, 9
moulding 26, 27

Nestlé, Henri 19
Nigeria 9

Pelican, The 12
Pepys, Samuel 13
Peter, Daniel 19
Phoenicians 4

Quakers 20
Quetzalcoatl 8

Rowntree, Isaac 15

Silk Road, The 4, 5
Steele, Sir Richard 14

tempering 26, 27
Tenochtitlan 7, 9
Terry, Joseph 15

Van Houten 16
Vera Cruz 7
Victoria, Queen 16

West Africa 22
West Indies 5
White's 13, 14

xocolatl 3, 8, 9

FASCINATING FACT

If all the Crunchies eaten in one year were laid end to end, they would stretch a distance of 14 000 miles.